MW01124153

365
Reflections on
FATHERS

Also available from Adams Media Corporation

365 Reflections on Daughters
365 Reflections on Fathers
365 Reflections on Grandmothers
365 Reflections on Love & Friendship
365 Reflections on Mothers
365 Reflections on Sisters
365 Women Who Made a Difference
365 Reflections on Men

365
Reflections on
FATHERS

Selected and arranged by
Dahlia Porter and Gabriel Cervantes

Adams Media Corporation
Holbrook, Massachusetts

Published by Adams Media Corporation
260 Center Street, Holbrook, MA 02343

ISBN: 1-58062-009-4

Printed in Canada.
J I H G F E D C B A

Library of Congress Cataloging-in-Publication Data
365 reflections on fathers / selected and arranged
by Dahlia Porter and Gabriel Cervantes.
p.   cm.
ISBN 1-58062-009-4 (paperback)
1. Fathers–Quotations. I. Porter, Dahlia. II. Cervantes, Gabriel.
PN6084.F3A155   1998
891'.5511–dc21   97-47046
CIP

Photo by ©TSM/Elizabeth Hathon

This book is available at quantity discounts for bulk purchases.
For information, call 1-800-872-5627 (in Massachusetts, 781-767-8100).

Visit our home page at http://www.adamsmedia.com

Contents

❦

My Father

*E*very day of my life has been a gift from him. His lap had been my refuge from lightning and thunder. His arms had sheltered me from teenage heartbreak. His wisdom and understanding had sustained me as an adult.

—*Nellie Pike Randall*

*M*y father . . . lived as if he were poured from iron, and loved his family with a vulnerability that was touching.

—*Mari E. Evans*

$\mathcal{M}$y father was two men, one sympathetic and intuitional, the other critical and logical; altogether they formed a combination that could not be thrown off its feet.

—*Julian Hawthorne,*
of his father, Nathaniel

$\mathcal{I}$ remember being upset once and telling my dad I wasn't following through right, and he replied, "Nancy, it doesn't make any difference to a ball what you do after you hit it."

—*Nancy Lopez*

$\mathcal{M}$y fondest and earliest memory of my father is being able to get in his lap and sit. I still to this day sit in his lap, and he loves it. I don't think you're ever too old for that.

—*Holly Heston,*
of her father, Charlton

For Richard Carney Porter
who will always be an inspiration in my life

$\mathcal{H}$e opened the jar of pickles when no one else could. He was the only one in the house who wasn't afraid to go into the basement by himself. He cut himself shaving, but no one kissed it or got excited about it. It was understood that when it rained, he got the car and brought it around to the door. When anyone was sick, he went out to get the prescription filled. He took lots of pictures . . . but he was never in them.

—*Erma Bombeck*

$\mathcal{M}$y dad is the backbone of our family. Any problem that I've ever had, he's always been there for me.

— *Whitney Houston*

The history, the root, the strength
of my father is the strength we
now rest on.

—*Carolyn M. Rodgers*

I modeled myself on my father. And this much at least was worthy of admiration: nothing downed his spirits for long.

—*Elaine Feinstein*

When I think of my father, the memories that bubble to the surface are not policy or politics. They are the man who opened a child's imagination, who taught her to be a good horsewoman and to always get back on when I fell off.

—*Patti Davis,*
of her father, Ronald Reagan

$\mathcal{I}$ was not close to my father, but he was very special to me. Whenever I did something as a little girl — learn to swim or act in a school play, for instance — he was fabulous. There would be a certain look in his eyes. It made me feel great.

—*Diane Keaton*

To this day I cannot see a bright daffodil, a proud gladiola, or a smooth eggplant without thinking of Papa. Like his plants and trees, I grew up as a part of his garden.

—*Leo Buscaglia*

$\mathcal{B}$eaming like a lesser god,
  He bounced upon the
    earth he trod.

—*May Sarton,*
of her father

14 365 REFLECTIONS ON FATHERS

*M*y dear father! When I remember
him, it is always with his arms
open wide to love and comfort me.

—*Isobel Field*

*W*hen someone who knew my
father says I'm like him, I
feel flattered. He was a shy,
undemonstrative man, but good natured
with a great, whimsical sense of humor.

— *Paul Newman*

$\mathcal{W}$hen I was fourteen, my father
was so ignorant I could
hardly stand to have the old man
around. But when I got to be twenty-
one, I was astonished at how much he
had learned in seven years.

—*Mark Twain*

$\mathcal{M}$y father died many years ago, and yet when something special happens to me, I talk to him secretly not really knowing what he hears, but it makes me better to half believe it.

—*Natasha Josefowitz*

$\mathcal{I}$ guess the only thing that's important is that he was my father. He was some guy, my Dad. Some guy.

—*Jack Lemmon*

$\mathcal{T}$he memory of Papa—tall, dark-haired, with a neatly trimmed mustache, smiling, warm and loving—is still vivid in my mind. It will never fade.

—*Leo Buscaglia*

What strikes me as odd now is how my father managed to get across to me without those heart-to-hearts which I've read about fathers and sons having in the study or in the rowboat or in the car. . . . Somehow I understood completely how he expected me to behave, in small matters as well as large, even though I can't remember being given any lectures about it beyond the occasional, undramatic, "You might as well be a mensch."

—*Calvin Trillin*

$\mathcal{O}$f course there were areas of safety;
nothing could get at me if I curled
up on my father's lap, holding on to his
ear with one thumb tucked into it. . . .
All about him was safe.

—*Naomi Mitchson*

One night at about two o'clock in the morning my father caught a man stealing bananas from our backyard. He went over to the man with his machete, took the bananas, cut the bunch in half and said, "Here, you can have it." And then he said, "From now on, if you need anything from the back of our house, come to the front."

— *Chi Chi Rodriguez*

There must've been hundreds of people cheering at some of those track meets, but my father's voice always found me. A simple "That's it, kid" and my feet grew wings.

—*Madison Riley*

$\mathcal{I}$ used to feel that all I ever did was take from my father: "Dad, my heater's not working." "Dad, I need help building the shed." "Dad, can you lend me money for a car?" Now he has a computer. Things are evening up quickly.

—*Den Schlaf*

*W*henever I try to recall that long
ago first day at school only one
memory shines through: my father held
my hand.

—*Marcelene Cox*

$\mathcal{M}$y father's sonorous voice brought Kipling's "great gray-green, greasy Limpopo River all set about with fever-trees" snaking right to the foot of my bed.

— *Victoria Secunda*

$\mathcal{I}$t was my father's hand that
opened wide
The door to poetry, where printed line
Became alive.

—*Helen Bean Byerly*

*T*here are a couple of pictures of the two of us that are of great sentimental value. In one, he's holding a bat in his left hand and has me comfortably balanced on his right shoulder. Some of the photos may be faded, but the memories of the happy times we spent together will always remain sharp and clear in my mind.

—*Dorothy Ruth Picone,*
of her father, Babe Ruth

As my poor father used to say
In 1863,
Once people start on all this Art
Goodbye moralitee!
And what my father used to say
Is good enough for me.

—*Sir A. P. Herbert*

$\mathcal{M}$y father was a romancer and most of my memories of him are colored I fear by an untruthfulness that I must have caught from him like one of the colds that ran around my family.

—*Mary McCarthy*

$\mathcal{I}$n my dreams
my father is
always kind.

—*Paul Gunn Allen*

*H*ow would I describe my father?
Cool. He's cool. He's learned.
He knows a lot of stuff.

— *Wynton Marsalis*

$\mathcal{M}$y father used to say that we must
surrender our youth to purchase
wisdom. What he never told me was
how badly we get cheated on the
exchange rate.

—*Morris West*

$\mathcal{M}$y father was as compulsive and efficient as I am. At Saturday morning breakfast, he would give each of us a list of chores that we had to get done for the day before any free time. My mother would get very upset when she got a list.

—*David Fissel*

$\mathcal{D}$own in the bottom of my
childhood my father
stands laughing.

— *Tove Ditlevsen*

$\mathcal{G}$ laughed once in my father's face,
and he laughed, and the
two laughters
locked like bumpers
that still rust between us.

—*Linda Pastan*

$\mathcal{P}$apa was a man of brimstone and hot fire, in his mind and in his fists, and was known . . . as the champion of all fist fighters. He used his fists on sharks and fakers, and all to give his family nice things.

— *Woody Guthrie*

$\mathcal{H}$e was generous with his affection, given to great, awkward, engulfing hugs, and I can remember so clearly the smell of his hugs, all starched shirt, tobacco, Old Spice and Cutty Sark. Sometimes I think I've never been properly hugged since.

—*Linda Ellerbee*

$\mathcal{H}$e [my father] also emphasized that a man's dignity lives after him; it's what you contribute to this world that matters, not what you take out of it. The essence of love is not to be loved but to give love.

—*Ricardo Montalban,*
of his father

$\mathcal{H}$e was strong rather than profound . . . I often wonder about him. In my struggle to be a writer, it was he who supported me and backed me and explained me . . .

—*John Steinbeck*

$\mathcal{M}$y father was the most dominant
person in our family and
in my life.

—Jimmy Carter

$\mathcal{M}$y father was very strong. I don't agree with a lot of the ways he brought me up. I don't agree with a lot of his values, but he did have a lot of integrity, and if he told us not to do something, he didn't do it either.

—*Madonna*

$\mathcal{H}$e had the precious gift of being deaf when convenient. Many people took this for absent-mindedness, but it was rather his faculty for concentrating on what suited him . . . in order to grasp reality better he limited his perceptions to a few definite things.

—*Jean Renoir*

$\mathcal{F}$ather was never late. Indeed, punctuality was his eleventh commandment. He saw lateness as a signal to the boss that you didn't care about your job, a potentially suicidal misstep. "If you're to be there at seven," he lectured me, "you be there at six forty-five. And you don't go to the water bucket more than once an hour."

—*Dan Rather*

$\mathcal{M}$y dad was relaxed and casual and believed in living in the present and having a good time. He had a full life and enjoyed himself no matter what happened.

—*Bing Crosby*

There is magic in the moment, for when I open my eyes and see my sons in the place where my father once sat, I feel an invisible bond between our three generations, an anchor of loyalty linking my sons to be the grandfather whose face they never saw but whose person they have already come to know through this most timeless of all sports, baseball.

—*Doris Kearns Goodwin*

As for my father, few souls are less troubled. He can be simply pleased with us, pleased that we exist, and, from the vantage point of his wondrously serene old age, he contemplates our lives almost as if they were books he can dip into whenever he wants. His back pages, perhaps.

—*Angela Carter*

Fathers
and
Daughters

*W*hen a father gives his daughter an emotional visa to strike out on her own, he is always with her. Such a daughter has her encouraging, understanding daddy in her head, cheering her on—not simply as a woman but as a whole, unique human being with unlimited possibilities.

— *Victoria Secunda*

$\mathcal{T}$here is something like a line of gold thread running through the man's words when he talks to his daughter, and gradually over the years it gets to be long enough for you to pick up in your hands and weave into a cloth that feels like love itself.

—*John Gregory Brown*

$\mathcal{T}$he most important relationship
within the family, second only
to that of husband and wife, is the
relationship between father
and daughter.

—*David Jeremiah*

$\mathcal{I}$n love to our wives there is desire, to our sons there is ambition; but in that to our daughters there is something which there are no words to express.

—*Joseph Addison*

*A*rthur always had his arms around [his daughter] Camera. When he talked about her, his face would light up like the stars in the sky. He showed more feeling for his daughter than I had seen him show his whole life.

—*Horace Ashe*

I've been trying to think of the last
thing that awed me. . . . The only
thing I can come up with is the birth of
my daughter almost five years ago.

—*Leonard Pitts Jr.*

*W*hat joy upon the honored
sire must come
When showing forth the wisdom of his
child!
Lo, she is fair and pure and undefiled
Thanks, thanks to her, the gladness of
his home!

—*Rahel Morpurgo*

$\mathcal{T}$he father of a daughter is nothing but a high-class hostage. A father turns a stony face to his sons, berates them, shakes his antlers, paws the ground, snorts, runs them into the underbrush, but when his daughter puts her arm over his shoulder and says, "Daddy, I need to ask you something," he is a pat of butter in a hot frying pan.

—*Garrison Keillor*

$\mathcal{I}$ can do one of two things. I can be
president of the United States, or
I can control Alice. I cannot possibly
do both.

—Theodore Roosevelt

One word of command from me is obeyed by millions . . . but I cannot get my three daughters . . . to come down to breakfast on time.

—*Viscount Archibald Wavell*

$\mathcal{T}$he thing to remember about
fathers is, they're men.

—*Phyllis Diller*

$\mathcal{H}$e wrapped his little daughter in his large
Man's doublet, careless did it fit or no.

—Elizabeth Barrett Browning

$\mathcal{I}$ know my weak points, but I've thought I was attractive since I was a girl because my father thought I was. He must have been kind. I was always cute, but I was a butterball.

—*Dana Delany*

When it comes to little girls, God the father has nothing on father, the god. It's an awesome responsibility.

—*Frank Pittman*

$\mathcal{I}$ remember being at a point below his knees and looking up past the vast length of him. He was six foot three; his voice was big. He was devastatingly attractive — even to his daughter as a child. . . . His voice was so beautiful, so enveloping. He was just bigger and better than anyone else.

—*Anjelica Huston*
of her father, John

$\mathcal{W}$hat a dreadful thing it must be to have a dull father.

—*Mary Mapes Dodge*

$\mathcal{F}$athers seem powerful and overwhelming to their daughters. Let her see your soft side. Express your feelings and reactions. Tell her where you came from and how you got there. Let her see that you have fears, failures, anxious times, hurts, just like hers, even though you may look flawless to her.

—*Stella Chess*

$\mathcal{I}$ wanted him to cherish and approve of me, not as he had when I was a child, but as the woman I was, who had her own mind and had made other choices.

—*Adrienne Rich*

If Daddy must be dethroned for daughter to begin to accept him as merely mortal, so, too, must a father give up the idea that his daughter will forever be his worshipping little girl—a process that can be peaceful or, more often than not, turbulent.

—*Victoria Secunda*

$\mathscr{G}$ want something from Daddy that he is not able to give me. . . . It is only that I long for Daddy's real love: not only as a child, but for me — Anne, myself.

—Anne Frank

𝒩othing is dearer to an old father
than a daughter. Sons have
spirits of higher pitch, but they are not
given to fondness.

—*Euripides*

$\mathcal{S}$he climbed into my lap and curled into the crook of my left arm. I couldn't move that arm, but I could cradle Ashtin in it. I could kiss the top of her head. And I could have no doubt that this was one of the sweetest moments of my life.

—*Dennis Byrd,*
of his daughter

Fathers are what give daughters away to other men who aren't nearly good enough, so they can have grandchildren who are smarter than anybody's.

—*Paul Harvey*

The father of the bride is a pitiable creature . . . always in the way—a sort of backward child—humored but not participating in the big decisions.

—*Dean Acheson*

The meaningful role of the father of the bride was played out long before the church music began. It stretched across those years of infancy and puberty, adolescence and young adulthood. That's when she needs you at her side.

— *Tom Brokaw*

$\mathcal{M}$any fathers waste hours of precious time in the vain attempt to convince their daughters they shouldn't care what the boys think. They say things like, "You've got plenty of time for boys later." Come on. Get real, Dad.

—*Nicky Marone*

$\mathcal{A}$ father is always making his baby into a little woman. And when she is a woman he turns her back again.

—*Enid Bagnold*

$\mathcal{I}$t isn't that I'm a weak father, it's just that she's a strong daughter.

—*Henry Fonda*

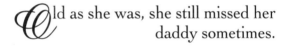

$\mathcal{O}$ld as she was, she still missed her
daddy sometimes.

—*Gloria Naylor*

$\mathcal{W}$omen's childhood relationships
with their fathers are
important to them all their lives.

—*Stella Chess*

What matters to me is not how I look, but the person inside, the one who grew up as — and is forever proud to be — the daughter of Bill Shepard.

—*Cybill Shepard*

Fathers
and Sons

The axe rang sharply 'mid those
forest shades
Which from creation toward the sky
had tower'd
In unshorn beauty. There, with
vigorous arm,
Walked a bold emigrant, and by his side
His little son, with question and
response
Beguil'd the time.

—Lydia Howard Sigourney

*E*very father knows at once too much and too little about his own son.

—*Fanny Fern*

$\mathcal{I}$ find that I'm moved by the silent memory of Dad and me silently competing at baseball on a dead-end street in a backwater Jersey town. There is something clean and elastic about it, and I look forward to speaking that mute language of men with my own son.

— *William Plummer*

$\mathcal{O}$f you can give your son only one
gift, let it be enthusiasm.

—*Bruce Barton*

$\mathcal{T}$he sooner you treat your son as a man, the sooner he will be one.

—*John Dryden*

$\mathcal{H}$e that does not bring up his son to some honest calling and employment, brings him up to be a thief.

—*Jewish proverb*

$\mathcal{M}$ost fathers would rather see their sons dead than either cultivated or devout.

—*Louis Auchincloss*

You don't raise heroes, you raise sons. And if you treat them like sons, they'll turn out to be heroes, even if it's just in your own eyes.

— *Walter Schirra Jr.*

$\mathcal{E}$very parent is at some time the
father of the unreturned
prodigal, with nothing to do but
keep his house open to hope.

—*John Ciardi*

We think our fathers fools, so wise
we grow;
Our wiser sons, no doubt, will
think us so.

—*Alexander Pope*

$\mathcal{H}$aving a child ends forever a man's boyhood, if not his boyishness. Having a child means that the son has, in a real sense, become his father. Sons are for fathers the twice told tale.

—*Victoria Secunda*

$\mathcal{H}$e may be president, but he still
comes home and swipes
my socks.

—*Joseph P. Kennedy,
on his son, John*

$\mathcal{F}$athers and sons are much more
considerate of one another
than mothers and daughters.

—*Friedrich Nietzsche*

$\mathcal{I}$ recently turned fifty, which is young for a tree, midlife for an elephant, and ancient for a quarter miler, whose son now says, "Dad, I just can't run the quarter with you anymore unless I bring something to read."

—*Bill Cosby*

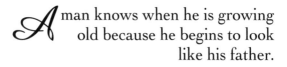

$\mathcal{A}$ man knows when he is growing old because he begins to look like his father.

—*Gabriel García Márquez*

$\mathcal{N}$o man is responsible for his father. That is entirely his mother's affair.

—*Margaret Turnbull*

$\mathcal{N}$early every man is a firm believer in heredity until his son makes a fool of himself.

—*Herbert V. Prochnow*

$\mathcal{I}$t is funny. The two things men are most proud of are the things that any man can do, and does in the same way—being drunk and being the father of their son.

—*Gertrude Stein*

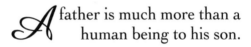

A father is much more than a
human being to his son.

— *Thomas William Simpson*

To a young boy, the father is a giant
from whose shoulders you can
see forever.

—*Perry Garfinkel*

'Tis happy for him, that his father
was before him.

—*Jonathan Swift*

$\mathcal{H}$e that will have his son have
respect for him and his
orders must himself have a great
reverence for his son.

—*John Locke*

$\mathcal{T}$he father who does not teach his
son his duties is equally guilty
with the son who neglects them.

—*Confucius*

Sir Walter, being strangely surprised
and put out of his countenance at
so great a table, gives his son a damned
blow over the face. His son, as rude as
he was, would not strike his father, but
strikes the gentleman that sat next to
him and said, "Box about: 'twill come to
my father anon."

— *John Aubrey*

$\mathscr{O}$f the relationship of father to son
could really be reduced to
biology, the whole earth would blaze
with the glory of fathers and sons.

—*James Baldwin*

$\mathcal{P}$erhaps host and guest is the
happiest relation for father
and son.

—*Evelyn Waugh*

$\mathcal{H}$is father watched him across the gulf of years, which always must divide a father from his son.

—*J. P. Marquand*

The time not to become a father is
eighteen years before a
world war.

—*E. B. White*

$\mathcal{I}$n peace the sons bury the fathers,
but in war the fathers
bury the sons.

— *Croesus*

$\mathcal{F}$or thousands of years, fathers and sons have stretched wistful hands across the canyon of time.

—*Alan Valentine*

*L*EONTINE: An only son, sir, might
expect more indulgence.
CROAKER: An only father, sir, might
expect more obedience.

— *Oliver Goldsmith*

Sons have always a rebellious wish to be disillusioned by that which charmed their fathers.

—Aldous Huxley

$\mathcal{A}$ man's desire for a son is usually nothing but the wish to duplicate himself in order that such a remarkable pattern may not be lost to the world.

—*Helen Rowland*

What was silent in the father speaks in the son; and often I found the son the unveiled secret of the father.

—*Friedrich Nietzsche*

$\mathcal{H}$e followed in his father's
footsteps, but his gait
was somewhat erratic.

—*Nicola Bentley*

The worst misfortune that can happen to an ordinary man is to have an extraordinary father.

—*Austin O'Malley*

We were walking through the woods—I was no more than eight—when a branch snapped back and hit my face. As I started to bawl, my father got a disgusted look and said "You'll never make a Marine." . . . After that moment he realized his path might not be mine, he was the most caring and supportive man I have ever known.

—*Jack Finley*

It was a big deal one day long ago in August when your father had cleaned his finger nails for the occasion and then you made him the proudest Dad in all the world. Every boy was supposed to come into the world equipped with a father whose prime function was to be our father and show us how to be men. He can escape us, but we can never escape him. Present or absent, dead or alive, real or imagined, our father is the main man in our masculinity.

— *Frank Pittman*

$\mathcal{D}$ad, you couldn't have done it better. You're actually pretty amazing especially because I'm fully aware of the demanding brat I was.

—*John Travolta,*
in a letter to his father

For a boy to reach adulthood feeling that he knows his father, his father must allow his emotions to be visible — hardly an easy task when most males grow up being either subtly or openly taught that this is not acceptable behavior. A father must teach his son that masculinity and feelings go hand in hand.

—*Kyle Pruett*

$\mathcal{U}$ntil you have a son of your own
. . . you will never know the
joy, the love beyond feeling that
resonates in the heart of
a father as he looks
upon his son.

—*Kent Nerburn*

$\mathcal{I}$t is not flesh and blood but the heart that makes us fathers and sons.

Friedrich von Schiller

Children

$\mathcal{I}$t was then that I glimpsed the baby's head for the first time. . . . It was still a mere dot, but for me it was a spot of eternity.

—*Carl Jones*

$\mathcal{I}$ know fame and power are for the birds. But then suddenly life comes into focus for me. And, ah, there stand my kids. I love them.

—*Lee Iacocca*

"*I* never could suffer infants, but this kid is different than all I've seen," is an expression often heard from proud young fathers.

—*Miles Franklin*

We have to give ourselves—men in particular—permission to really be with and get to know our children. The premise is that taking care of kids can be a pain in the ass, and it is frustrating and agonizing, but also gratifying and enjoyable. When a little kid says, "I love you, Daddy," or cries and you comfort her or him, life becomes a richer experience.

—*Anonymous*

$\mathcal{B}$efore I got married I had six theories on children; now I have six children and no theories.

—John Wilmot

$\mathcal{T}$hen I discovered that my son had learned something new. For the first time, he was able to give a proper kiss, puckering up his lips and enfolding my face in his arms. "Kees Dada," he said as he bussed me on the nose and cheeks. No amount of gratification at work could have compensated for that moment.

—*Donald H. Bell*

A man finds out what is meant by a spitting image when he tries to feed cereal to his infant.

—*Imogene Fay*

One father can support twelve
children, but twelve
children cannot support one father.

—*French proverb*

$\mathcal{A}$ new father quickly learns that his child invariably comes to the bathroom at precisely the times when he's in there, as if he needed company. The only way for this father to be certain of bathroom privacy is to shave at the gas station.

— *Bill Cosby*

$\mathcal{I}$t is a wise father that knows his
own child.

— *William Shakespeare*

$\mathcal{I}$t is a wise child that owes his own father.

—*Carolyn Wells*

$\mathcal{T}$he debt of gratitude we owe our mother and father goes forward, not backward. What we owe our parents is the bill presented to us by our children.

—*Nancy Friday*

The roaring of the wind is my wife
and the stars through the
window pane are my children.

—*John Keats*

Almost every time I watch my daughters playing near me, especially in a physical way, an unusual feeling takes hold of me. I do not identify with the big smiling male whose offspring play at his feet, although I do expect to feel like this, looking at their tiny bodies and my own big one. On the contrary, I feel small and open. I feel as if the three of us are learning independently how to be dependent on one another.

—*Mordechai Rimor*

$\mathcal{M}$en just don't "get" that the reason to become involved is for ourselves. Doing more with our children won't simply make women happier or keep them "off our back," but will create a deeper, more positive connection with the kids.

—*Ron Taffel*

$\mathcal{T}$he most important thing a father
can do for his children is to love
their mother.

— *Theodore Hesburgh*

$\mathcal{N}$ot only do our wives need our support, but our children need our deep involvement in their lives. If this period [the early years] of primitive needs and primitive caretaking passes without us, it is lost forever. We can be involved in other ways, but never again on this profoundly intimate level.

—*Augustus Y. Napier*

A little child, a limbering elf
singing, dancing to
itself. . . . Make such a vision to the
sight, as fills a father's eyes with light.

—*Samuel Taylor Coleridge*

$\mathcal{T}$he first handshake in life is the greatest of all: the clasp of an infant's fist around a parent's finger.

—*Mark Beltaire*

Safe, for a child, is his father's hand,
holding him tight.

—*Marion C. Garretty*

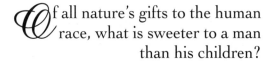

Of all nature's gifts to the human race, what is sweeter to a man than his children?

— *Cicero*

$\mathcal{T}$o show a child what has once delighted you, to find the child's delight added to your own, so that there is now a double delight seen in the glow of trust and affection, this is happiness.

—*J. B. Priestly*

*B*lessed indeed is the man who
hears many gentle
voices call him father.

—*Lydia Maria Child*

Daddy's favorite tools are numbered among a child's favorite toys. Every kid wants to get her hands on Dad's retracting tape measure and his hammer. One father told me that his kids had taken over his under-car creeper as their favorite riding toy and he has trouble getting it back when he wants to change the oil.

—*St. Claire Adams Sullivan*

$\mathcal{H}$ow can one say no to a child?
How can one be anything
but a slave to one's own flesh
and blood?

—*Henry Miller*

$\mathcal{B}$uying a stereo is merely a father's practice for the Big Buy: a car. When a child requests a car, a father will wish that he were a member of some sect that hasn't gone beyond the horse.

— *Bill Cosby*

A child enters your home and for the next twenty years make so much noise you can hardly stand it. The child departs, leaving the house so silent, you think you are going mad.

—*John Andrew Holmes*

A llow children to be happy in
their own way, for what
better way will they ever find?

—*Samuel Johnson*

$\mathcal{I}$ have found that the best way to
   give advice to your children is
to find out what they want and then
            advise them to do it.

—*Harry S Truman*

154 ❧   365 REFLECTIONS ON FATHERS

$\mathcal{D}$on't demand respect, as a parent. Demand civility and insist on honesty. But respect is something you must earn — with kids as well as adults.

— *William Attwood*

$\mathcal{M}$ore broadly across time and cultures, it seems, one perennial piece of advice to fathers has been the importance of acting tenderly toward their children.

—*David Blankenhorn*

$\mathcal{T}$he best brought up children are those who have seen their parents as they are. Hypocrisy is not the parents' first duty.

—*George Bernard Shaw*

$\mathcal{W}$hen children sound silly, you will always find that it is in imitation of their elders.

—*Ernest Dimnet*

$\mathcal{R}$aising children is part joy and
part guerilla warfare.

—*Ed Asner*

$\mathscr{P}$arents ought, through their own behavior and the values by which they live, to provide direction for their children. But they need to rid themselves of the idea that there are surefire methods which, when well applied, will produce certain predictable results. Whatever we do with and for our children ought to flow from our understanding of our feelings for the particular situation and the relation we wish to exist between us and our child.

—*Bruno Bettelheim*

*P*arents lend children their experience and a vicarious memory; children endow their parents with a vicarious immortality.

—*George Santayana*

$\mathcal{H}$appy that man whose children
make his happiness in life
and not his grief.

—*Euripides*

$\mathcal{W}$e have seen that men are learning that work, productivity, and marriage may be very important parts of life, but they are not its whole cloth. The rest of the fabric is made of nurturing relationships, especially those with children— relationships which are intimate, trusting, humane, complex, and full of care.

—*Kyle D. Pruett*

$\mathcal{R}$omance fails us and so do friendships, but the relationship of parent and child, less noisy than all others, remains indelible and indestructible, the strongest relationship on earth.

— *Theodore Reik*

*W*hen you have children, you
begin to understand what
you owe your parents.

—*Japanese proverb*

$\mathcal{C}$hildren aren't happy with nothing
to ignore, and that is what
parents are created for.

—*Ogden Nash*

A baby has a way of making a man out of his father and a boy out of his grandfather.

—*Angie Papadakis*

$\mathcal{H}$ow pleasant it is for a father to sit at his child's table. It is like an aged man reclining under the shadow of an oak he had planted.

—*Sir Walter Scott*

Influence

There have been many times when I thought people might be better singers or better musicians or prettier than me, but then I would hear Daddy's voice telling me to never say never, and I would find a way to squeeze an extra inch or two out of what God had given me.

—*Barbara Mandrell*

*N*one of you can *ever* be proud enough of being the *child* of SUCH a Father who has not his *equal* in this world—so great, so good, so faultless. Try, all of you, to follow in his footsteps and don't be discouraged, for to be *really* in everything like him *none* of you, I am sure, will ever be. Try, therefore, to be like him in *some* points, and you will have *acquired a great deal.*

—*Queen Victoria*

What a father says to his children
is not heard by the world, but
it will be heard by posterity.

—*Jean Paul Richter*

$\mathcal{M}$y father got me strong and
straight and slim
And I give thanks to him.
My mother bore me glad and sound
and sweet,
I kiss her feet!

—*Marguerite Wilkinson*

Today's sons can emulate Joe Montana, Kirby Puckett, Wayne Gretzsky or Michael Jordan. Yet Dad's way has some extra appeal— he represents our personal destiny. Few father's will ever threaten Joe DiMaggio's hitting streak, but to a son Dad's way far outweighs social recognition.

—*Jerrold Lee Shapiro*

*M*any people now believe that if fathers are more interested in raising children than they were, children and sons in particular will learn that men can be warm and supportive of others as well as be high achievers. Thus, fathers' involvement may be beneficial not because it will help support traditional male roles, but because it will help to break them down.

—*Joseph Pleck*

*C*hildren have never been very good
at listening to their elders, but
they have never failed to imitate them.

—*James Baldwin*

*W*ords have an awesome impact.
The impression made by a
father's voice can set in motion an entire
trend of life.

—*Gordon MacDonald*

$\mathcal{I}$ chance to talk a little wild,
forgive me;
I had it from my father.

— *William Shakespeare*

We live in the past to an
astonishing degree,
the myth we live by, the presumptions
we make. Nobody can look in the mirror
and not see his mother or father.

—*E. L. Doctorow*

$\mathcal{A}$s a parent, you will often serve as an inadequate example to your child. A child will model himself after you in many areas: how you deal with frustration, settle disagreements and cope with not being able to have the things that you want, to name just three.

—*Lawrence Balter*

Even if society dictates that men and women should behave in certain ways, it is fathers and mothers who teach those ways to children—not just in the words they say, but in the lives they lead.

—*Augustus Y. Napier*

*C*hildren are natural mimics—they act like their fathers or mothers in spite of every attempt to teach them good manners.

—*Anonymous*

*W*hy do I have to be an example
for your kid? *You* be an
example for your own kid.

—*Bob Gibson*

Setting a good example for your
children takes all the fun out
of middle age.

— *William Feather*

$\mathcal{M}$y father taught me to read from one of those first-grade readers. "Oh my," said Dick. "See Spot run." My father reacted right away, taking a bright red pencil, crossing out the "Oh my's" and writing in "Odds bodkins," "Gadzooks," "Gorblimey," and such all down the page. It was a revelation. It was the opposite of boring. The possibilities seemed endless and wonderful and I think it was at that moment I became a writer.

—*Gordon Chaplin*

By looking at us, listening to us, hearing us, respecting our opinions, affirming our value, giving us a sense of dignity, he was unquestionably our most influential teacher.

—*Leo Buscaglia*
from Papa, My Father

Love

No man can possibly know what life means, what the world means, what anything means, until he has had a child and loves it. And then the whole universe changes and nothing will ever seem exactly as it seems before.

—*Lafcadio Hearn*

$\mathcal{T}$here is something ultimate in a
father's love, something that
cannot fail, something to be believed
against the whole world.

—*Frederick W. Faber*

$\mathcal{H}$e loves his children not because everything in them is lovely and according to his liking, but because there is a real incomprehensible bond which is stronger than fiction.

—*Leroy Brownlow*

$\mathcal{M}$en love their children, not
because they are
promising plants, but because they
are theirs.

—*Charles Montagu*

$\mathcal{I}$ do not love him because he is good, but because he is my little child.

—*Rabindranath Tagore*

*W*hat children expect from grown-ups is not to be "understood," but only to be loved, even though this love may be expressed clumsily or in sternness. Intimacy does not exist between generations—only trust.

—*Carl Zucker*

The Fountaine of parent's duties is Love. . . . Great reason there is why this affection should be fast fixed towards their children. For great is that paine, cost and care, which parents must undergoe for their children. But if love be in them, no paine, paines, cost or care will seeme too much.

— *William Gouge*

*A*ll the feeling which my father could not put into words was in his hand—any dog, child or horse would recognize the kindness of it.

—*Freya Stark*

$\mathcal{W}$hen you are a father, and you
hear your children's voices,
you will feel that those little ones are
akin to every drop in your veins; that
they are the very flower of your life and
you will cleave so closely to them that
you seem to feel every movement that
they make.

— *Honoré de Balzac*

Give a little love to a child, and you
    will get a great deal back.

—*John Ruskin*

In a man whose childhood has known caresses and kindness, there is always a fibre of memory that can be touched by gentle issues.

—*George Eliot*

$\mathcal{L}$et us now praise famous men, and
our fathers that begat us.

— *The Bible*

$\mathscr{D}$ads don't need to be tall and broad
shouldered and clever. Love
makes them so.

—*Pam Brown*

Fathers! blessed word.

—*Maria S. Cummins*

$\mathcal{I}$t's only when you grow up, and step back from him, or leave him for your own career and your own home—it's only then that you can measure his greatness and fully appreciate it. Pride reinforces love.

—*Margaret Truman,*
of her father, Harry S

To her the name of father was
another name for love.

—*Fanny Fern*

$\mathcal{M}$y earliest recollections are of being dressed up and allowed to come down to dance for a group of gentlemen who applauded and laughed as I pirouetted before them. Finally, my father would pick me up and hold me high in the air. He dominated my life as long as he lived, and was the love of my life for many years after he died.

— *Eleanor Roosevelt*

Our father, while he lived, had cast magic over everything, for us as well as for her. He held his love up over us like an umbrella and kept off the trouble that afterwards came down on us, pouring cats and dogs!

—*Mary Lavin*

$\mathcal{B}$e kind to thy father, for when
thou wert young,
Who loved thee so fondly as he?
He caught the first accents that fell from
thy tongue,
And joined in thy innocent glee.

—*Margaret Courtney*

$\mathcal{N}$o music is so pleasant to the ears
as that word—father.

—*Lydia Maria Child*

*T*he best portion of a
good man's life,
His little nameless, unremembered acts
Of kindness and love.

— *William Wordsworth*

A man's fatherliness is enriched as much by his acceptance of his feminine and childlike strivings as it is by his memories of tender closeness with his own father. A man who has been able to accept tenderness from his father is able later in life to be tender with his own children.

—*Louise J. Kaplan*

In the love of a brave and faithful man there is always a strain of maternal tenderness; he gives out again those beams of protecting fondness which were shed on him as he lay on his mother's knee.

—*George Eliot*

*I*t's a wonderful feeling when your father becomes not a god but a man to you—when he comes down from the mountain and you see he's this man with weaknesses. And you love him as this whole being, not as a figurehead.

—*Robin Williams*

$\mathcal{Y}$ou don't have to deserve your
mother's love. You have to
deserve your father's.
He's more particular.

—*Robert Frost*

Discipline

$\mathcal{C}$hildren need love, especially when
they do not deserve it.

—*Harold S. Hubert*

As a father I had some trouble finding the words to separate the person from the deed. Usually, when one of my sons broke the rules or a window, I was too angry to speak calmly and objectively. My own solution was to express my feelings, but in an exaggerated, humorous way: "You do that again and you will be grounded so long they will call you Rip Van Winkle II," or "If I hear that word again, I'm going to braid your tongue."

—*David Elkind*

It is a wise child that knows its own father, and an unusual one that unreservedly approves of him.

—*Mark Twain*

$\mathcal{M}$y father was frightened of his mother. I was frightened of my father and I am damned well going to see to it that my children are frightened of me.

—*George V*

I'll meet the raging skies,
But not an angry
father.

— *Thomas Campbell*

They were always reading the law
to her at home, which might not
have been so bad if her father and
mother had read from the same book.

—*Jessamyn West*

When a father is indulgent, he is more indulgent than a mother. Little ones treat their mother as the authority of rule, and their father as the authority of dispensation.

—*Frederick W. Faber*

The best time to tackle a minor
problem is before it
grows up.

—*Ray Freedman*

*T*he relationship of a parent with a teenager is shot through with ambiguities and hypocrisies, large and small—the child's dependance and resentment, the parent's self-indulgence and prohibitions. But somewhere within this uneasy mix, in the best of families . . . both parent and child know which lines should not be crossed; the child's sense of privacy, the parent's sense of propriety. A delicate balance preserved until, as adults, both sides can either laugh about it or forget it.

—*Richard North Patterson*

The thing that impresses me most
about America is the way
parents obey their children.

—*Edward, Duke of Windsor*

$\mathcal{M}$ost parents feel the keen embarrassment of having the infant misbehave . . . and they are apt to offer a tacit apology and a vague self-defense by sharply reprimanding the child in words that are meant to give the visitor the idea that they—the parents—never *heard or saw* such conduct before, and are now frozen with amazement.

—*Agnes H. Morton*

*A*lways end the name of your child with a vowel, so that when you yell, the name will carry.

—*Bill Cosby*

How easy a father's tenderness recalled, and how quickly a son's offenses vanish, at the slightest word of repentance!

—*Molière*

$\mathcal{F}$athers are blind to the faults
of their daughters.

— *Proverb*

*P*ronouncements have been raised
to a fine art by daddies, who use
them to deflect a messy personal
encounter while keeping everything
under control.

—*Signe Hammer*

*G*overn a small family as you
would cook a small
fish, gently.

—*Chinese proverb*

$\mathcal{I}$t is better to bind your child to you
by a feeling of respect, and by
gentleness, than by fear.

— Terence

$\mathcal{A}$n atmosphere of trust, love and humor can nourish extraordinary human capacity. One key is authenticity: parents acting as people, not as roles.

—*Marilyn Ferguson*

Expectations

$\mathcal{I}$t is impossible to please the whole world and your father as well.

—*Jean de la Fontaine*

$\mathcal{I}$ phoned my dad to tell him I had stopped smoking. He called me a quitter.

—*Steven Pearl*

$\mathcal{E}$veryone expects to go further than his father went; everyone expects to be better than he was born and every generation has one big impulse in its heart—to exceed all other generations of the past in all the things that make life worth living.

—William Allen White

*I*t is the family's expectations
that will make father into
his best and biggest self.

—*Samuel S. Drury*

We criticize mothers for closeness. We criticize fathers for distance. How many of us have expected less from our fathers and appreciated what they gave us more? How many of us always let them off the hook?

—*Mary Kay Blakely*

*F*athers see babies as potentially grown-up—they are more likely than mothers to transform their perception of their newborn into fantasies about the adult it will become, and about the things that they (father and child) will be able to do together when the infant is much older.

—*Dorothy Burlingham*

$\mathcal{E}$very father expects his boy to do the things he wouldn't do when he was young.

—*Kin Hubbard*

$\mathcal{F}$athers and mothers have lost the
idea that the highest aspiration
they might have for their children is for
them to be wise . . . specialized
competence and success are all that they
can imagine.

—*Allan Bloom*

$\mathcal{T}$he most important thing about
our time together was this:
whatever his politics or view of the role
of women, he never made me think there
was anything I couldn't do.

—Susan Kenney,
of her father

The Need for a Father

*F*athers have a special excitement about them that babies find intriguing. At this time in his life an infant counts on his mother for rootedness and anchoring. He can count on his father to be just different enough from his mother. Fathers embody a delicious mixture of familiarity and novelty.

—*Louise J. Kaplan*

$\mathcal{F}$athers represent another way of
looking at life—the possibility
of an alternative dialogue.

—*Louise J. Kaplan*

Our father presents an optional set of rhythms and responses for us to connect to. As a second home base, he makes it safer to roam. With him as an ally—a love—it is safer, too, to show that we're mad when we're mad at our mother. We can hate and not be abandoned, hate and still love.

—*Judith Viorst*

$\mathcal{I}$ cannot think of any need in childhood as strong as the need for a father's protection.

—*Sigmund Freud*

$\mathcal{C}$hildren want to feel instinctively
that their father is behind them
as solid as a mountain, but, like a
mountain, is something to look up to.

—*Dorothy Thompson*

*F*ather, dear Father, come home
with me now,
The clock in the steeple strikes one;
You said you were coming right home from
the shop,
As soon as your day's work was done;
Our fire has gone out, our house is all dark,
And mother's been waiting since tea,
With poor Benny so sick in her arms,
And no one home to help but me.
Come home! Come home! Come home!
Please, Father, *dear* Father, come home.

—*Henry Claywork*

*Y*our children need your presence
more than your presents.

—*Jesse Jackson*

$\mathcal{I}$ believe that I'm letting my kids see that a man can be tender, sensible, warm, attentive to feelings, and present, just plain there. That's important to me, because I didn't get any of that from my own father, and I am realizing now how much I missed it.

—*Anonymous*

$\mathcal{O}$f fathers who fear fathering and run away from it could only see how a little fathering is enough. Mostly, the father just needs to be there.

—*Frank Pittman*

That is natural enough when
nobody has had fathers
they begin to long for them and then
when everybody has had fathers they
begin to do without them.

—*Gertrude Stein*

$\mathcal{T}$o tolerate the trend of
fatherlessness is to
accept the inevitability of continued
social recession.

—David Blankenhorn

254 🌣 365 R<small>EFLECTIONS ON</small> F<small>ATHERS</small>

$\mathcal{A}$s a substitute father for hundreds of youths over the past thirteen years, I have yet to encounter a young person in difficulty whose trouble could not be traced to the lack of a strong father image in his home.

—*Paul Anderson*

The sound of his father's voice was a necessity. He longed for the sight of his stooped shoulders as he had never, in the sharpest of his hunger, longed for food.

—*Marjorie Kinnan Rawlings*

Being a Father

*B*y profession I am a soldier and take pride in that fact. But I am prouder — infinitely prouder — to be a father.

—*Douglas MacArthur*

$\mathcal{I}$ felt something impossible for me to explain in words. Then when they took her away, it hit me. I got scared all over again and began to feel giddy. Then it came to me — I was a father.

—*Nat King Cole*

$\mathcal{A}$ father is a person who is forced
to endure childbirth without an
anesthetic.

—*Robert C. Savage*

A man prides himself on his strength — but when his child is born he discovers that strength is not enough, and that he must learn gentleness.

— *Pam Brown*

$\mathcal{I}$'d been cast in the part of my life . . . but I'd never heard of the leading man. I was definitely playing a supportive role; Lydia and I rated only feature billing. Still, I've never had a better part, and only once one as good — in the sequel. I was to be a father.

— *Charlton Heston*

*B*eing a father
   Is quite a
      bother,
But I like it, rather.

—*Ogden Nash*

$\mathcal{L}$ike many fathers, he had a favorite ritual: to put his whole family in the car and drive somewhere. It didn't matter where — what mattered was that he was behind the wheel.

— *Signe Hammer*

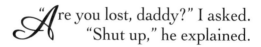

"*A*re you lost, daddy?" I asked.
"Shut up," he explained.

—*Ring Lardner*

What was it, this being "a good father"? To love one's sons and daughters was not enough; to carry in one's bones and blood a pride in them, a longing for their growth and development—this was not enough. One had to be a ready companion to games and hikes and outings, to earn from the world this accolade. The devil with it.

—*Laura Z. Hobson*

$\mathcal{I}$t is much easier to become a father
than to be one.

—*Kent Nerburn*

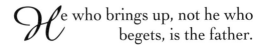

*H*e who brings up, not he who
begets, is the father.

— *The Bible*

To conceive a child, my father told
me, is as simple as blowing a
feather off your knee.

—*John Cheever*

$\mathcal{D}$on't make a baby if you can't
be a father.

—*National Urban League slogan*

To be a successful father . . . there's
one absolute rule: when you have
a kid, don't look at it for the
first two years.

—*Ernest Hemingway*

To become a father is not hard,
    To be a father is, however.

— *Wilhelm Busch*

The good-enough father is not simply a knight in shining armor galloping to the occasional rescue; he is there through the good times and bad, insisting on and delighting in his paternity every pleasurable and painful step of the way.

— *Victoria Secunda*

$\mathcal{S}$cary. That may be the most perfect
word there is to describe what it's
like to be a parent.

—*D. L. Stewart*

The pressures of being a parent are equal to any pressure on earth. To be a conscious parent, and really look to the little being's mental and physical health, is a responsibility which most of us, including me, avoid most of the time because it's too hard.

—*John Lennon*

*T*he kind of man who thinks that helping with the dishes is beneath him will also think that helping with the baby is beneath him, and then he certainly is not going to be a very successful father.

—*Eleanor Roosevelt*

$\mathcal{I}$ loved those years of being Mr. Mom. One of the saddest days in my life was when Jennifer said, "Dad, I can wash my own hair."

—*Billy Crystal*

"*D*o you like being a parent—you know, being a father, having children and all?" Linnet once asked me. "Yes," I said, after a moment. "It's like dancing with a partner. It takes a lot of effort to do it well. But when it's done well it's a beautiful thing to see."

—*Gerald Early*

The daily arguments over putting away the toys or practicing the piano defeat us so easily. We see them coming and yet they frustrate us time and time again. In many cases, we are mothers and fathers who have managed budgets and unruly bosses and done difficult jobs well through sheer tenacity and dogged preparation. So why are we unable to persuade someone three feet tall to step into six inches of water at bathtime?

—*Cathy Rindner Tempelsman*

$\mathcal{I}$ don't want to be a good pal, I want to be a father.

—*Clifton Fadiman*

$\mathcal{P}$arents teach in the toughest school in the world — The School for Making People. You are the board of education, the principal, the classroom teacher, and the janitor.

—*Virginia Satir*

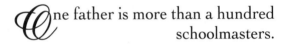

$\mathcal{O}$ne father is more than a hundred
schoolmasters.

—English proverb

*D*ad, if you really want to know what happened in school, then you've got to know exactly who's in the class, who rides the bus, what project they're working on in science, and how your child felt that morning. . . . Without these facts at your fingertips, all you can really say is "So how was school today?" And you've got to be prepared for the inevitable answer — "Fine." Which will probably leave you wishing that you'd never asked.

—*Ron Taffel*

$\mathcal{M}$y dad was always there for me and my brother, and I want my kids to have the same kind of dad—a dad they will remember. Being a dad is the most important thing in my life.

—*Kevin Costner*

*S*herman made the terrible discovery
      that men make about their fathers
sooner or later . . . that the man before him
    was not an aging father but a boy, a boy
    much like himself, a boy who grew up and
       had a child of his own and, as best he
    could, out of a sense of duty and, perhaps
    love, adopted a role called Being a Father
      so that his child would have something
         mythical and infinitely important: a
    protector, who would keep a lid on all the
chaotic and catastrophic possibilities of life.

— *Tom Wolfe*

$\mathcal{D}$ads are stone skimmers, mud wallowers, water wallopers, ceiling swoopers, shoulder gallopers, upsy-downsy, over and through, round about wooshers. Dads are smugglers and secret sharers.

—*Helen Thomas*

*T*here are to us no ties at all just in being a father. . . . It's the practice of parenthood that makes you feel that, after all, there may be something in it.

—*Heywood Broun*

Fatherhood

I thought I never wanted to be a father. A child seemed to be a series of limitations and responsibilities that offered no reward. But when I experienced the perfection of fatherhood, the rest of the world remade itself in my eyes.

—*Kent Nerburn*

$\mathcal{F}$atherhood, for me, has been less a job than an unstable and surprising combination of adventure, blindman's buff, guerilla warfare and crossword puzzle.

—*Frederic F. van de Water*

[Fatherhood] is the single most creative, complicated, fulfilling, frustrating, engrossing, enriching, depleting endeavor of a man's adult life.

—*Kyle D. Pruett*

$\mathcal{I}$ had heard all those things about fatherhood, how great it is. But it's greater than I'd ever expected—I had no idea Quinton would steal my heart the way he has. From the minute I laid eyes on him, I knew nobody could ever wrestle him away from me.

—*Burt Reynolds*

$\mathcal{F}$atherhood, like marriage, is a constant struggle against your limitations and self-interests. But the urge to be a perfect father is there, because your child is the perfect gift.

—*Kent Nerburn*

$\mathcal{F}$atherhood is pretending the present
you love the most is
soap-on-a-rope.

—*Bill Cosby*

The advent of Father's Day in America has inspired the advertisement pages of the magazines to suggestions for brightening the life of this poor underprivileged peon. "Buy him an outboard run-about speedboat fourteen feet long with a sixty foot beam," say the magazines. "Buy him a synchromatic wristwatch, water and shock resistant. Buy him a fishing rod seven foot long with reinforced ferrules and large-capacity spinning Beachcomber reel," say the magazines, knowing perfectly well that if he gets anything, it will be a tie with pink horses on a blue background.

—*P. G. Wodehouse*

$\mathcal{O}$nce you've been launched into parenthood, you'll need all your best skills, self-control, good judgement and patience. But at the same time there is nothing like the thrill and exhilaration that come from watching that bright, cheerful, inquisitive, creative, eccentric and even goofy child you have raised flourish and shine. That's what keeps you going, and what, in the end, makes it all worthwhile.

—*Lawrence Balter*

The power of this experience can never be explained. It is one of those joyful codings that rumbles in the species far below understanding. When it is experienced it makes you one with all men in a way that fills you with warmth and harmony.

—*Kent Nerburn,*
of fatherhood

$\mathcal{E}$veryone tells me that I've become
much mellower since I
became a father.

—*Burt Reynolds*

$\mathcal{I}$ looked at my daughters, and my boyhood picture, and appreciated the gift of parenthood, at that moment, more than any other gift I have ever been given. . . . Who else would think your insignificant and petty life so precious in the living, so rich in its expressiveness, that it would be worth partaking of what you were, to understand what you are?

—Gerald Early

$\mathcal{P}$arenthood is not an object of
appetite or even desire. It is
an object of will. There is no appetite for
parenthood; there is only purpose or
intention of parenthood.

—R. G. Collingwood

$\mathcal{M}$y fatherhood made me
understand my
parents and honor them more
for the love they gave.

—*Kent Nerburn*

$\mathcal{T}$here are times when parenthood
seems nothing more than
feeding the mouth that bites you.

—*Peter De Vries*

*P*arenthood remains the single
greatest preserve
of the amateur.

—*Alvin Toffler*

$\mathcal{P}$arenthood isn't a picnic. Dad may
work from sun to sun, but as a
father he's never done.

— *William D. Wilkins*

$\mathcal{P}$aternity is a career imposed on you without an inquiry into your fitness.

—*Adlai E. Stevenson*

The toughest part of parenthood has nothing to do with putting food on the table, clothes in the closet, or tuition money in the bank. The toughest part of parenthood is never knowing if you're doing the right thing.

—*D. L. Stewart*

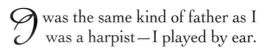

$\mathcal{I}$ was the same kind of father as I was a harpist — I played by ear.

—*Harpo Marx*

$\mathscr{O}$f there's one thing parenthood has
taught me it's that naive mistakes
do not bad parents make. Bad parents
have decidedly bad attitudes.

—*John Rosemond*

The American father . . . passes his life entirely on Wall Street and communicates with his family once a month by means of a telegram in cipher.

— *Oscar Wilde*

$\mathcal{I}$t has always been economically and
politically important for men to
know that they are the fathers
of their children.

—*Louise Bernikow*

$\mathcal{T}$he most important domestic
challenge facing the U.S. at
the close of the twentieth century is the
re-creation of fatherhood as a vital social
role for men.

—*David Blankenhorn*

There was a time when a father amounted to something in the United States. He was held with some esteem in the community; he had some authority in his own household; his views were sometimes taken seriously by his children; and even his wife paid heed to him from time to time.

—*Adlai E. Stevenson*

$\mathcal{F}$atherhood ought to be emphasized
as much as motherhood. The idea
that women are solely responsible for
deciding whether or not to have babies
leads on to the idea that they are also
responsible for bringing the children up.

—*Shirley Williams*

$\mathcal{T}$he ivory tower school of the men's movement has some strong feelings about the fatherhood role. According to its adherents, not only are men capable of upstaging women in baking banana bread and folding diapers, but nurturing, cooing, soothing, and everything short of breast-feeding should be included in the daddy repertory.

—Ira Victor

$\mathcal{S}$ometimes my wife complains that she's overwhelmed with work and just can't take one of the kids, for example, to a piano lesson. I'll offer to do it for her, and then she'll say, "No, I'll do it." We have to negotiate how much I trespass into that mother role—it's not given up easily.

—*Anonymous*

Defining and celebrating the New Father are by far the most popular ideas in our contemporary discourse on fatherhood. Father as close and nurturing, not distant and authoritarian. Fatherhood as more than bread winning. Fatherhood as new-and-improved masculinity. Fathers unafraid of feelings. Fathers without sexism. Fatherhood as fifty-fifty parenthood, undistorted by arbitrary gender divisions or stifling social roles.

— *David Blankenhorn*

Parenting

$\mathcal{A}$ man doesn't have to have all the answers—children will teach him how to parent them, and in the process will teach him everything he needs to know about life.

—*Frank Pittman*

$\mathcal{P}$arenting is the one area of my life
where I can feel incompetent,
out of control and like a total failure all
of the time.

—*Anonymous*

A king realizing his incompetence, can either delegate or abdicate his duties. A father can do neither. If only sons could see the paradox, they would understand the dilemma.

—*Marlene Dietrich*

$\mathcal{F}$athers are something else. They always give up their turn by saying something like, "Go ask your mother. She knows about things like that."

—*Mary Kuczkir*

$\mathcal{S}$ince mothers are more likely to take children to their activities—the playground, ballet or karate class, birthday parties—they get a chance to see other children in action. . . . Fathers usually don't spend as much time with other people's kids; because of this, they have a narrower view of what constitutes "normal" behavior, and therefore what should or shouldn't require parental discipline.

—*Ron Taffel*

To raise good human beings it is not only necessary to be a good mother and a good father, but to have had a good mother and father.

—*Marcelene Cox*

$\mathcal{B}$ecoming Father the Nurturer rather than just Father the Provider enables a man to fully feel and express his humanity and his masculinity. Fathering is the most masculine thing a man can do.

—*Frank Pittman*

*F*athering makes a man, whatever his standing in the eyes of the world, feel strong and good and important, just as he makes his child feel loved and valued.

—*Frank Pittman*

$\mathcal{N}$o matter how calmly you try to referee, parenting will eventually produce bizarre behavior, and I'm not talking about the kids. *Their* behavior is always normal.

—*Bill Cosby*

$\mathcal{T}$hree stages in a parent's life:
nutrition, dentition, tuition.

—*Marcelene Cox*

Fathers should be neither seen nor
heard. That is the only proper
basis for family life.

—*Oscar Wilde*

$\mathcal{I}$n a number of other cultures, fathers are not relegated to babysitter status, nor is their ability to be primary nurturers so readily dismissed. . . . We have evidence that in our own society men can rear and nurture their children competently and that men's methods, although different from those of women, are imaginative and constructive.

—*Kyle D. Pruett*

The guys who fear becoming fathers don't understand that fathering is not something perfect men do, but something that perfects the man. The end product of child raising is not the child but the parent.

—*Frank Pittman*

$\mathscr{A}$lthough we consider parents the king and queen of a family, we think they must respect their subjects now, if only to avoid the guillotine later.

—*Marguerite Kelly and Elia Parsons*

Selective ignorance, a cornerstone of child rearing. You don't put kids under surveillance: it might frighten you. Parents should sit tall in the saddle and look upon their troops with a noble and benevolent and extremely nearsighted gaze.

—*Garrison Keillor*

$\mathcal{J}$f the new American father feels
bewildered and even defeated,
let him take comfort from the fact that
whatever he does in any fathering
situation has a fifty percent chance of
being right.

—*Bill Cosby*

There are only two kinds of parents. Those who think their offspring can do nothing wrong, and those who think they can do nothing right.

—*Miles Franklin*

$\mathcal{A}$nything which parents have not
learned from experience they
can now learn from their children.

—*Anonymous*

If you are a parent it helps if
you are a grownup.

—*Eda J. LeShan*

$\mathcal{T}$he mark of a good parent is that
he can have fun while
being one.

—*Marcelene Cox*

$\mathcal{W}$hen I was away from home and missing my children, I asked myself why I didn't show my approval and enjoyment of them more when I was with them, when it would do them—and me—a lot of good. But I don't think I was ever able to take my own advice.

The psychological explanation for this is that we crabby perfectionists were started in that direction in our own childhood by the frequent criticism of our parents; it is very difficult to overcome the compulsion to repeat what was done to us.

—*Benjamin Spock*

$\mathcal{L}$et children know you are human.
It's important for children to see
that parents are human and make
mistakes. When you're sorry about
something you've said or done,
apologize! It is best when parents
apologize in a manner that is
straightforward and sincere.

—*Saf Lerman*

$\mathcal{I}$t will help us and our children if we can laugh at our faults. It will help us tolerate our shortcomings and it will help our children see that the goal is to be human, not perfect.

—*Neil Kurshan*

$\mathcal{I}$t seems to me that upbringings have themes. The parents set the theme, either explicitly or implicitly, and the children pick it up , sometimes accurately and sometimes not so accurately. . . . The theme may be "Our family has a distinguished heritage that you must live up to" or "No matter what happens, we are fortunate to be together in this lovely corner of the earth" or "We have worked hard so that you can have the opportunities we didn't have."

—*Calvin Trillin*

To maintain a joyful family requires much from both the parents and the children. Each member of the family has to become, in a special way, the servant of the others.

—*Pope John Paul II*

*I*n colonial America, the father was the primary parent. . . . Over the past two hundred years, each generation of fathers has had less authority than the last. . . . Masculinity ceased to be defined in terms of domestic involvement, skills at fathering and husbanding, but began to be defined in terms of making money. Man had to leave home to work. They stopped doing all the things they used to do.

—*Frank Pittman*

So often, as the septuagenarian
reflects on life's rewards, we
hear that, "in the final analysis" of
money, power, prestige, and marriage,
fathering alone was what "mattered."

—*Kyle Pruett*

Guidance: What My Father Taught Me

$\mathcal{I}$ watched a small man with thick
calluses on both hands work
fifteen and sixteen hours a day . . . a man
who came here uneducated, alone,
unable to speak the language, who
taught me all I needed to know about
faith and hard work by the simple
eloquence of his example.

—*Mario Cuomo,*
of his father

$\mathcal{P}$arents have become so convinced that educators know what is best for children that they forget that they themselves are really the experts.

—*Marian Wright Edelman*

$\mathcal{H}$e always said, "Babe, pay your own way. Don't owe anybody anything." And that's the way I've lived.

—*Lily Tomlin,*
of her father

$\mathcal{I}$ just owe everything to my father [and] it's passionately interesting for me that the things that I learned in a small town, in a very modest home, are just the things that I believe have won the election.

—*Margaret Thatcher*

*M*y father, who was in politics, told me to remain a bit mysterious. A good friend and father figure to him gave him this advice. It makes people wonder about you, draws them to you as we are all drawn to a mystery.

—*Joe Mills*

$\mathcal{N}$ever get sick, Hubert,
there isn't time.

—*Hubert Humphrey's father*

$\mathcal{W}$hen I was a child my father
taught me to put up my
fists like a boy and to be prepared to
defend myself at all times.

—*Camille Paglia*

$\mathcal{I}$ worked hard and made my own way, just as my father had. And just, I'm sure, as he hoped I would. I learned, from observing him, the satisfaction that comes from striving and seeing a dream fulfilled.

—*Sigourney Weaver*

$\mathcal{I}$ remember my father's final lesson.
My boy will learn by what I am
and what I do far more than I
will tell him.

—*Norman Lewis Smith*

$\mathcal{A}$ good name and good advice is all your dad can give you.

—*Harry S Truman*

ad gave me two pieces of advice. One was "No matter how good you think you are, there are people better than you." But he was an optimist too; his other advice: "Never worry about rejection. Every day is a new beginning."

—*John Ritter*

*E*ven if fathers are more benignly helpful, and even if they spend time with us teaching us what they know, rarely do they tell us what they feel. They stand apart emotionally: strong perhaps, maybe caring in a nonverbal, implicit way; but their internal world remains mysterious, unseen, "What are they really like?" we ask ourselves. "What do they feel about us, about the world, about themselves?"

—*Augustus Y. Napier*

$\mathcal{M}$y heart is happy, my mind is free
I had a father who talked
with me.

—*Hilda Bigelow*

$\mathscr{D}$ad is sort of a laid back type, quiet and soft spoken. He believes in a good education, being a good person and having good morals. He instilled those values in me.

—*Ralph Brennan*

$\mathcal{I}$n my younger and more vulnerable
years my father gave me some
advice I've been turning over in my head
ever since.

—*F. Scott Fitzgerald*

$\mathcal{D}$on't limit a child to your own learning, for he was born in another time.

—*Jewish proverb*

In order to live a good and clean life
my father has taught me six
basic rules:
If I don't do it, then you don't do it.
No one knows the truth but your
conscience and God.
You are never a failure as long as you
give it your best.

Do not forget your culture.
Do not do something just because
I am around.
Education and honesty are two of the
most important things that you
should have.

—*Dagem Hailemarian*

All that we [old poets] can do is keep our hearts as fresh as we may; to bear ever in mind that a father can guide a son but some distance on the road, and that how wisely he guides the sooner (alas!) must he lose the fair companionship and watch the boy run on.

— *Sir Arthur Quiller-Couch*

$\mathcal{M}$y father always told me: You have the rest of your life to figure out what you want to do with the rest of your life.

—*John Beilenson*

Finding the perfect balance is getting harder and harder. We need to teach our children to be cautious without imparting fear, to learn right from wrong without being judgmental, to be assertive but not pushy, to stick to routines without sacrificing spontaneity, and to be determined but not stubborn.

— *Fred G. Gosman*

The most important thing that parents can teach their children is how to get along without them.

—*Frank Clark*

A wise father teaches skills.
Courage. Concentration
on the job in hand. Self-discipline.
Encourages enthusiasm. A spirit of
enquiry. Gentleness. Kindliness.
Patience. Courtesy. And love.

—*Pam Brown*

I talk and talk and talk, and I haven't taught people in fifty years what my father taught me by example in one week.

—*Mario Cuomo*

$\mathcal{D}$ad often said, "A man that doesn't pick up a penny that's laying on the ground won't ever amount to much." And if I'm not mistaken, the statement was prefaced by, "I remember my dad always saying . . ." So I'm the third (at least) generation to have received this wisdom.

—*Ric Anderson*

$\mathcal{D}$ad taught me to never settle for anything less than what I want. I think that's what made him so great. He always promotes that image of being such a tyrant, but the truth is, there couldn't be a sweeter father.

— *Victoria Preminger*

$\mathcal{M}$y father taught me to be independent and cocky, and free thinking, but he could not stand it if I disagreed with him.

—*Sara Maitland*

$\mathcal{M}$y father told me that you have to
be true to yourself before you
can give your best to others—
professionally and personally.

—*Nancy Wilson*

$\mathcal{I}$ learned from the example of my father that the manner in which one endures what must be endured is more important than the thing that must be endured.

—*Dean Acheson*

$\mathcal{W}$e were very poor, so my father worked two jobs at a time, sometimes three. So he wasn't home that much. On Christmas morning we would have to wait upstairs while he finished his milk deliveries before going down to open our presents. He took the time to do things with his kids. I think he taught by example, rather than by direct advice.

—*Sam Wynkoop*

$\mathcal{T}$rain a child in the way he should go, and when he is old he will not depart from it.

— *The Bible*

$\mathcal{M}$y best training came
from my father.

— *Woodrow Wilson*

$\mathcal{M}$y prescription for success is based on something my father always used to tell me: you should never try to be better than someone else, but you should never cease trying to be the best that you can be.

—*John Wooden*

"There's no such word as 'can't.'" . . .
If my father said something was
so, then that's the way it was, but how
could there not be such a word as "can't"
if I could hear and see and say it? —
though eventually I realized it was
another way of saying, "Never give up."

—*Susan Kenney*

$\mathcal{M}$y father taught me to be honest, to do the best job I could do, and to be fair to whomever I was dealing with. Whenever I worked for anyone, he always insisted I see the job through. He would not let me quit until the job was finished. He taught me good manners and how to be a gentleman. After twenty-five years of marriage, I still hold the door for my wife.

—*Harry Steele*

$\mathcal{T}$here are only two lasting bequests
we can hope to give our children.
One of these is roots; the other, wings.

—*Hodding Carter*

Bibliography

A. K. Adams. *The Home Book of Humorous Quotations.* New York: Dood, Mead & Co., 1969.

Robert Andrews. *The Columbia Dictionary of Quotations.* New York: Columbia University Press, 1993.

Donald O. Bolander. *Instant Quotation Dictionary.* New York: Dell Publishing, 1972.

Eugene E. Brussell. *Dictionary of Quotable Definitions.* Englewood, New Jersey: Prentice Hall, 1970.

J. M. and M. J. Cohen. *The Penguin Dictionary of Quotations.* New York: Viking, 1960.

Catherine M. Edmonson. *365 Women's Reflections on Men.* Holbrook, Massachusetts: Adams Media Corporation, 1997.

Eugene Ehrlic and Marshall De Bruh, eds. *The International Thesaurus of Quotations.* New York: Harper Collins, 1996.

Helen Exley, ed. *The Best of Father Quotations*. New York: Exley Giftbooks, 1996.

Helen Exley, ed. *The Love Between Fathers and Daughters*. New York: Exley Giftbooks, 1995.

Susan Feuer. *For My Father*. Kansas City: Andrews and McMeel, 1996.

Susan Ginsberg, ed. *Family Wisdom: The 2,000 Most Important Things Ever Said About Parenting, Children, and Family Life*. New York: Columbia University Press, 1996.

Elizabeth Jakus. *For Dad*. White Plains, New York: Peter Pauper Press, 1992.

Rosalie Maggio, ed. *The New Beacon Book of Quotations by Women*. Boston: Beacon Press, 1996.

Frank N. Magill. *Magill's Quotation in Context*. New York: Harper & Row, 1965

Margaret Miner and Hugh Rawson. *The New International Dictionary of Quotations*. 2nd ed. New York: Signet, 1993.

Dierdre Mullane. *Words to Make My Dream Children Live.* New York: Doubleday, 1995.

Elaine Partnow. *The Quotable Woman 1800–1981.* New York: Facts on File, 1982.

Elaine Partnow. *The Quotable Woman Eve–1799.* New York: Facts on File, 1982.

Herbert V. Prochnow and Herbert V. Prochnow, Jr. *A Treasury of Humorous Quotations.* New York: Harper & Row, 1969.

William Safire and Leonard Safir. *Words of Wisdom.* New York: Simon and Schuster, 1989.

James B. Simpson. *Simpson's Contemporary Quotations.* New York: Harper Collins, 1997.

Carolyn Warner. *The Last Word.* Englewood, New Jersey: Prentice Hall, 1992.

Dad. Philadelphia: Running Press, 1997

With Love to a Special Father. Grand Rapids, Michigan: Fleming H. Revell, 1995.